Island of
Dark Horses

To Susan Cowby
and in Memory of Gwen Robson, 1919-92,
for their enthusiastic efforts to keep Bardsey/Enlli
as a place to live and work.

Royalties from this book will be donated to the Bardsey Island
Trust (Ymddiriedolaeth Enlli) for its work "to salvage what is left of
the traditional way of life of this unique community".

Island of
Dark Horses

Christine Evans

seren

seren
is the book imprint of
Poetry wales Press Ltd.
First Floor, 2 Wyndham Street,
Bridgend, Mid Glamorgan,
Wales, CF31 1EF

Cataloguing In Publication Data for this book
is available from the British Library

ISBN 1-85411-137-X

*The publisher acknowledges the finanical assistance of the
Arts Council of Wales*

Cover photograph of Bardsey island by Peter Hope Jones

Printed by The Cromwell Press
Melksham

Contents

7	Songline
7	Primal
8	Enlli
9	Meeting the Boat
11	Window, Dynogoch
12	Gannets
14	Waves
16	Morning Watch
18	Night Walkers
18	Island in Summer
19	Signals
20	Taking the Stain
21	Siblings
22	Island Children
24	Pulpit Enlli
26	Off Camera
26	Tide
27	Earthwork
28	Sounding
31	Grey Arms
32	Jane's Dream
34	A Cowrie Shell for Saiorse
36	Sevens
39	From the Stone
41	Encounter
43	Case History
43	Western Horizon
44	Next Day
46	On Retreat
47	Myxomatosis
48	Meanwhile, in Another Part of the Island
50	Stone
50	After the Storm
51	In the Hayfield

52   Nocturnal
54   Inside the Bubble
56   Broc Môr
58   Brenda and the Golden Snake
62   At the End of Summer
63   Watchers
64   Douglas
65   Keeping in Touch
67   Storm
69   Through the Weather Window
71   Llŷn
73   Island of Dark Horses

94   *Notes*
96   *Acknowledgements*

Songline

Under my own apple tree
in a warm, walled garden
on an island
at the extremity of a green peninsula
in an amniotic sea

I sit and read
of nomads

so all night I hear herds
grunt and shuffle,
breathe earth and leather
under a roof of antlers
and embroidered flowers.

Behind, the grasses wither.
Beyond, the passes
may be blocked with snow.
Here is sweet water, a ripening
green now. I wake

to light-filled island air
and it is so.

Primal

Before Dawn, ocean
is a vast breathing cradle
where the sky itself kneels.

Enlli

(for Ceri when she was ten)

We get to it through troughs and rainbows

falling and flying

rocked in an eggshell
over drowned mountain ranges.

The island swings towards us, slowly.

We slide in on an oiled keel.
Step ashore with birth-wet, wind-red faces
wiping the salt from our eyes
and notice sudden, welling
quiet, and how here the breeze
lets smells of growing things
settle and grow warm, a host of presences
drowsing, too fine-winged to see.

A green track, lined with meadowsweet.
Stone houses, ramparts to the weather.
Small fields that run all one way
to the sea, inviting feet
to make new paths to their own
discovered places.

After supper, lamplight
soft as the sheen of buttercups
and candle-shadow blossoming
bold on the bedroom wall.

Outside's a swirl of black and silver.
The lighthouse swings its white bird round
as if one day it will let go
the string, and let
the loosed light fly
back to its roost with the calling stars.

Meeting the Boat

Saturdays, we sit outside the boathouse
to wave goodbye... and watch the next lot land.

Some arrive well-wrapped
in the bubble of expectations
we might see punctured by a sharpening edge
of sense, if they stay long enough:

rucksacked, festooned with lenses,
the birdwatchers are triggered to observe
specific features of a habitat
where humans only incidentally intrude

while for the women (clammy, over-eager hands
and blood-drained faces) coming On Retreat
that to themselves they call a pilgrimage
the island, all of us, are in soft focus.

Families returning spring ashore
with cries like raiders'. The sons begin
to kick a plastic float or to throw stones.
Claude tells the lobstermen what bait to use.

Most new ones step ashore subdued
with egos well restrained, on leash,
until they have their island image
steady and this landscape shrunk

to context. The dinghy ferries
threes or fours and strands them
on the beach without their wives
or suitcases. Ankle-deep, they stand bemused or bray
for contact. Infants clutch and whine.

Now the voyage of discovery, or just getting here
turns into a performance or a ritual
no-one told them to expect.
They lurch and blunder over thwarts, or scramble

weed-slimed rocks towards the patch of sand —
the cliff — the row of waiting faces.
In turn, each has to improvise a way
to make a meeting with our mustered forces.

Then we will form a chain to land the luggage.

Window, Dynogoch

A deep-set lens, this small-paned window
still holds a ripple of the sand
so the world shifts as you turn your head —
shivers, our son says, like a crystal
looking back in time, not telling futures

and through its cave mouth just this afternoon
surprised by summer's lowest tide
I saw the rocks, dark-slimy-haired, uncouth,
hump and crawl and haul themselves
back out of the warm shallows on to land.

We prop it open with a waveworn stick
sit high-pillowed late to watch
stars dancing on the moleskin sea
four fields away as the little owl cries.
Sleep is muffled with the curtains closed.

All night the lighthouse prints its sixteen squares
on the whitewashed wall and on our faces
throwing dark's doors wide
over and over, to welcome the waker,
holding land and sea and present steady.

Downstairs, a witch-tangle of branches
springs up the kitchen wall
the shadow of what's always there
between, looked through, too close to see.
Another blazing instant: then the dark.

I lie and watch the arcs go over
a white rock profile, beard of silver thrift.
Each morning seems somewhere we've landed
brushed as we are all night in sleep
by the tireless wings of travelling light.

Gannets

Gannets fall
as if fired back
by sky they have stretched
with their slow, strong wing-beats.

They swim up
in a smooth loose spiral
plumping the clearness
rhythmically under
them, kneading until the blue is
taut and trembling —

a cold, elated second, focussing.
One heartbeat, then turn
arrowheads down, folded back wings
plummeting down, plummeting in.

The black of each wingtip
sharp as a fin.

The dark water sends up its own wings
of white spray as it is pierced.
The bay vibrates with their soundings.

Far out on the west, their whiteness
signals the early simple message
sun, before any warmth
spills over the hunched shoulder
we were glad to lie against all night.

How high? A hundred feet, or more...
Depends how deep the shoal is feeding.

Until we tire of looking
they beat themselves a shaft of slippery air
like working up from sleep;
let themselves be sucked back down

to green drawling minutes under, and
being bounced out through
widening rings of effervescent light.
Gulping air again, and energy.

Over and over they plunge
straight down into the dark
to spear a glimpsed magnetic glitter.

Watching makes us hold our breath.

Waves

Take the easier walking by the water's edge
and watch the waves' white flowering
about your feet, as innocent
as watered milk, but with a strength at back
that lends their momentary webs
the confidence of frost
and drowns
heartbeat
with its own. Steps
not only make no sound;
infill of salt, all tracks dissolved.
Shore and sky wiped clean, over and over,
by the pulse and roar and pounding
like a great loom
mumbling
its endless dream,
a trance of blossoming
without rot, curdling without sour.
This is frontier country:
to walk here is to feel
perception quicken and the intellect
for once sit humbly with its dials
gone dark; to seem immense
as cumulus,
infinitesimal
as sandgrain in the suck
of each wave's gathering. Stand still
and the whole slow world spins
round you, blue and white and dazzling,
vortices of shine that glide and beckon
offering completion
unravelling
control.
Dark sea-tresses
strain back from graves beneath the sand.
In the fetch of the seventh further-reaching wave
shiver in the shell that will be flotsam;
watch energy becoming froth,

bright spray turn to scum, but
dry to a tracery
of old healed scars.

Morning Watch

Inside, the lighthouse is gloss-painted
Like prison or a hospital. Too hot.
The radio stammers, blurts, then hums.
Sport or men with guns mutter on a screen
All look at, no-one watches, in an acrid haze
Of Players' Number 6 or roll-your-owns.
Nestlé's Milk coffee, or floating Marvel,
Is the only indication you're offshore
(Formica buckling, tin teapot, pedal bin)
Till you catch reflections of the symmetry
Of a nursery tale — for there are three
Of everything — three chairs with thin foam
Cushions that slide down as soon
As sat on, three tea-towels, bookshelves;
Out in the garden, three lavatory cells
Three toolsheds, pigsties, garden plots gone wild

And three pale unfocussed sedentary men
Sleeping, eating, being awake
On or off according to a roster.

Baz steps out, shirt-sleeved, to do the Met
(which numbers on the weather form he'll tick)
Acres of white foam, the air
A wide blue yawn he slams in from:
Christ! It's cold enough out there —
Their laughter drowns the thrum of engines.

But sometimes, he's confided, in the small hours
Sneaking the white gate close behind him
He truants, leaving light in its tower cage
Where homing seabirds grunt and scream and fall
To tread salt turf springy with old roots
And stand like a captain in the wind
Reading the dark stretch of his deck
Sensing the night miles crossed
Till his heartbeat's only a flicker
His cigarette a brave red throb
On the seabed of the floating stars.

His daylight brain thinks it forgotten
But in off-duty dreams, a hundred miles
From sea, he feels the island dip and steady;
Glimpses the black walls building, pushed astern
Tumbling, crawling, gathering, re-gathering
Outrun, but following.

Night Walkers

The sea is
a great ear turned to listen.

Soft paws of cloud
knead the moon
the night sky purrs
and presses closer.

We tread soft as mist
so small the dark could breathe us in
our thoughts bleached paler
than dandelion seeds

so when the world stirs
and shifts its weight
we see the ocean flash with fire
twice cooled to silver

but not one of the three of us
points or cries out.

Island in Summer

Under the swollen moon
Its body throbs warm between
Water's shining wings.

Signals

Once, from wherever on the island
I set out, our paths would close.
As at a time agreed for meeting
our random walks must touch

and flow together in a shining curve
as though there was a flavour
in the air, a throb of earth at evening
our bodies learned to follow.

Now, we trail alone round Marks and Spencer
grow irritable searching;
all too often, pass on the wrong side
— *I was there, but later* —

as though some key to place and time
no longer meshes in a lock worn smooth.
In the space between your flesh and mine
the resonances blur and merge.

And yet in some ways still the same
as when we first slid home at night together
in the long cool stroke
the lighthouse smoothes on sea and pasture.

Twenty summers further on
you, attuned to every stone or
track-twist, still have to tell me
Wait till the beam comes round

and I forget to look out for my feet
gazing up at an inverted ocean
where shearwaters' white bellies swim
between pricked bubbles that are stars

night opening before us at each step
the great sky whirling and calling
stumbling back after midnight beside you

as I choose still to do.

Taking the Stain

Inherited from Averilda's kitchen
These plastic plates have had their day;
Make all our island meals an expedition
But, sturdy Bakelite, defy attempts
To smash and throw away. Some mainland woman
Discarded them a generation since.
They belong with chipped enamel bowls and the
      white buckets
We used to carry milk or water in.

I tell myself they're unhygienic, cracked,
And others have absorbed the stains
Of food shared years ago — the blackberries
Gwen and David picked in bucketfuls
One late September they were stormbound here.
(We haven't eaten bramble jelly since.)
Darkening tomato, from the pasta
I used to fill the kids with after fishing
And on this, the sepia explosions
Of mushroom prints. That long wet summer
They piled up everywhere. And the schoolboy
Who, furtive and exulting, took his shirt off
To fill it with the first we saw that season
Is in the South Atlantic now
And it is winter.
                Mushrooms —
So milky-pale, so here-and-gone
And yet the pattern of the spreading gills
Will not be lost, until I break it.

Siblings

'Ogof Morlas', Woodcut by Kim Atkinson

This might be the first fish
ever landed, so eagerly she hunkers
to absorb its glazing greens and bronzes
drinking in the small cold glitter
of the world beyond them they have snatched it from

while, patient, kneeling, he invents a ritual
stroking almost tenderly along the bone
to lay the white flesh open. Her eyes
dog every exploration of the blade.

So many sharpnesses surround them.
They have climbed out of the shadowed gully
to where the rocks still flex and clench and tumble
back. The sea-cave that they shivered from
boomed and echoed with fierce gouging surges.

Outside the frame, the huge quivering ring
of the horizon shrugs. At its core
theirs is the only softness: the fish, even,
armour-plated against teeth.

Their world is one of still-unguarded thresholds.
The arch of her spine speaks of hunger
but in the secret pod her arms protect
already seed is ripening
the pattern for her daughters, and their daughters.

The dark pool yawns for them but sun
strokes warmth across her shoulders, feeds
the bunching muscles of the boy's forearms.
Will light their faces when they turn again to climb.

Island Children

Winter on the island now. No more
footfall in the field beside the bones
where Lleuddad's oratory stood;
child voices vanished, like the oats
shoulder-high in Carreg fields
like the tidy pride of lighthouse gardens
light leaping gold at dusk in every house.
Not even small ghosts hide in the bracken
hush whispers in the shadowy pews
or splash through pools on Pen Diban.
It's not memory but an electric pulse
that glances whitely from each window.

Gwyndon, storm-started, 1929
then Mary Greta, his sister, in Nant
followed by Mair, Nancy, Gwilym, Megan
Guto and Brenda; big Wil Cristin
and tiny Jane at Tŷ Pella. Gwynfor
last of the Dynogoch eight
named for the Swnt too white to cross,
Bessie and Wil from Carreg
and then the transitories in Plas —
little Billy Mark, boat-born, fearless
crawler between carthorse hooves
and his sisters, Joanne and Pauline.
From blitzed London, soft-spoken Roger
faced daily battles in the gorse bushes
sticking up for Vivienne and Keith
while his dad, Jack Harris, built a windmill.
Gwenda, Ronald, Jean and Robin
the Cristin children Brenda painted,
their cheekbones folded high like wings;
Ernest, last name on the register,
last child on the island until 1960
and Iain christened in the Abbey ruins.
Then Kim and Angus made the beaches theirs,
Patrick, first baby in Carreg Bach

for a century, and in Dynogoch, Colin Siôn.
Now, seventeen years on, a newer flowering:
the twins, fact-hungry Urien, and Saiorse,
Poppy, fearless Lois, Bun and Dafydd Bach
with sea-grey eyes and hair as bright
as rich red bracken under autumn sun.

May some of them be back next summer.

Pulpit Enlli

"There is a handsome pulpit in the chapel, carved in a valuable wood, a present from Egypt, I think. They had to build the chapel round it."

   Tomos O Enlli, by Jennie Jones, translated by Gwen Robson.

They are still blossoming, the cherubs
and the flowers with their flat oak petals
fewer after every summer tide
of tourists. When the door swings
shut on wind and sea, half a century's stone-stillness
nuzzles the warm pod
of your presence, chills with a breath
of sweetness too long trapped.
Lavender on stale linen. Rose petals in a jar.

And the pulpit cannot let the silence
speak, leave the space clear
for healing. It squats, a dark stump hiding
its own hollowness, and from it hang
gilt cherubs heavy as fungus
engorged and smug, the milk-fat
smoothness of their clinging limbs
tawdry but indifferent to time
that focuses these present cool
low-angling shafts of autumn sun.

1870: fourteen families
told to choose: stone harbour
or chapel, larger, more devoutly distant
from the main track of farmwork, gossip,
washing spread across the gorse to dry.
Trained to acceptance on this island
that keeps its back against the dawn
how could they see into a time
it was no longer God's will to have grown
two strong men from every house, to launch
and row the sort of boat they knew —
or picture their trim patchwork fields

rough as prairies, homes inaccessible
as America? Asked, in turn, to speak
how could they suddenly develop
defiant strategies of choice?

There are times in summer
when the ebb-tide, even here,
slows, heavy with reflected sweetness
in the fissures it has sucked out
on the west, when hayfields
thicken with flowers and stone houses
sun themselves, bland-faced as cats.
But this is a luxury, not to be
lived by. Sooner or later, salt
rasps the tender green. Crow and blowfly
wait. In the windthrashed bracken,
jagged edges, new-picked bones.

For photographs they wear, the last
gaunt, wide-bearded men
and their strong-browed women in dark clothes
the level unselfconscious gaze
of those who have survived
against the odds. I hope they thought
these stylized roses and winged infants
wonderful; that through the first long winter
their sons and daughters and the young ones gone
this promise of eternal succulence
could offer comfort as they sat
where I shiver in the empty pews
hearing only the wind whispering outside
only the horizons shuffling closer.

Off Camera

It is comparisons with Eden, effusions
on the quietness of Enlli
that make them smile off camera
the islanders returned by helicopter
to their birthplace for the day. Their faces say
this place was nothing special
more than all the hidden countries
of our childhood. The interviewer wants
hiraeth, the echoes of old loss
or an Ishmael resentment
to engage the audience and justify
his budget. But they do not seem
particularly thrilled
by the trick of sweeping back so smoothly. Even today
this white-ringed island is not inaccessible
to them: it is a real place
their minds return to regularly as the birds
to breed; the enduring pole
they measure progress from.
It is the mainland, they point out, themselves,
that have moved on.

Tide

First, seepage, then, flux:
as the great heart pumps and sucks
every inlet whispers.

Earthwork

All day, the tap and scrape of his spade
As I sit reading in the ginger ruins
Of my garden, or peel potatoes
With windows wide to let the evening cool
Breathe through the house.

    No more than a season afraid of being slow
    He is still digging out the stones
    And stacking turves against the sunset.
    Shoring up. Shaping a green surface
    That he hopes will knit and grow.

Each week he says will be his last
In the hayloft, self-castaway
For hours head-down in the shell sand
Sifting through the brightnesses
To string a necklace, brooches, out of bits.

    Or for a whole day drifts in his canoe
    Daring the glitter, testing the pull
    Of the tide and what ties him.
    Speaks to friends of having no more dreams;
    Finds faith enough to plant a hedge.

Now from the mainland, the east side
Of this island looks a charcoal husk
But some sharpness in the exhumed stones
Throws warm light back into his face
And the jagged edges seem already healing.

Sounding

Silences define us
Like the darknesses round stars....

The mist begins to thin: the foghorn's double echo ·
Takes twenty seconds fading into silence.

In the pause I hear
Sheep calling to their lambs that night is coming
A colt's companionable snorts
And the drugged sea breathing out.

Five days and nights it has been sounding
Crying our wrecking shore
To a world that seems oblivious
Left astern
The lighthouse splaying blind white fingers
Hexing a circle
That brims thick again.

Even light cannot scythe
Such lissomness, only stroke
Pearls from its strands.
Summer mist, a soft heaped fleece.

Again tonight we will lie
Curled at the heart of clamour
Where echoes well up:
Lulled by a pulse
So close it comes to seem our own.

(Half-awake in winter on the mainland
I hear the foghorn calling
As if from Cantre'r Gwaelod, land
Of all our drowning summers.)

Timing it makes the moment
Momentous, makes me recall
Contractions. And, after each

A glistening bag of quiet sounds
Opens, drying off around us.
Swaddled, the ground stretches and chuckles;
Glows in the tent of our seeing.
Somewhere in the sleeping cloud a warbler
Tries the rusty wheel of its song.

Twelve paces from my nose, the whole world
Blinks, or suddenly beyond a reef
Or a startle of foxgloves
Dissolves back into wet, thick air.
The sea croons, silky, pacified.
No boats leave or will arrive.

The first morning, it felt like bandages.
Now we strain for bearings closer in.
Some swell to cram the space they see
Knead loaves frenetically, count oyster-catcher chicks
Scrawl messages to people in the sun
Twiddle dials and turn the volume up.
Others burrow inward.

I hear generations of seamen grumble
Better a storm than fog
As if held on land they are afraid
They might take root. And first-time visitors
Such silence! But listen — even here
When wind and sea are still
There is the throb of heavy engines
Over the horizon, even on that empty ocean
The air crackles with messages
An incantation of yachts' names.

But peace, perhaps.
There is no quiet that matters
Except inside your head.

This is what the foghorn does:
Like a mantra, tugs awareness back
Continually to the centre.
Steadies minds to the lure

And quiet is a hole in the fog
The foghorn makes
A gate swinging open
To a known, fenced pasture
We can loose selves in

Not needing to clutch
The thread of our thought —

For most of us, an only time
To be still and catch a glimpse
Of our spinning
To be an echo from the centre
And go on unfolding

As all the smells of growing
Unfold moistly round us.

This afternoon
I trod a causeway through the clouds
That flexed and quivered like a great swan's wings
From the ridged spine of the mountain.
Dry grass crunched underfoot like snow.
Thistledown lifted on a thermal
And a well-shaft opened to the light
A shower of gold sparks dancing on the water

Unfathomable depth below
And in the shifting veils right over me
A growing incandescence like a torch
Approaching, or a great vague face
Bending into focus.

Then the thick stuff eddied back
Shaped itself a tunnel.
Through long corridors of bone, I heard
The fog signal again.

But not a tunnel: a cocoon.
Now curlew drawn home from the salt edge
Seed the steamy dusk with cries
Pointing to scoured upland and cold stars
While I slice bread, warm milk, my mind
Clouded like the window, wondering

What brinks, what late-summer vistas
We are all ripening towards
As we wait to see, wait
For the sun
To burn a way through.

Jane's Dream

She never dreamed an island, but a garden
formally planned, held firm within
warm brick walls. Repeatedly she explored
winding walks and tree caverns
in all its seasons in the lee of time.

Lambing time, mid bitter March. All day
a struggle against wind, north-easterly.
No shelter, spatter and drag
with each step. Sky and land conspiring
to a cold grey dissolution, and the sea
wrinkling in a snarl. Lambs sank
before they could be licked, ewes
wild and wary. One at North End
stamped over twins curled dead as stones together.

Sleep folded round her. She was walking
past thyme flowering in a patchwork
of warm scents and through a Gothic archway
from sunlight into shade, into profusion.
Clematis and white jasmine scrambled through
a huge old apple and a weeping pear
cascading in a cloud of foam. Chamomile,
white lilies, foxgloves, roses — *Margaret Merrill*
she knew from pictures, and *Belle de Crecy* — all
with a newborn gloss, their outlines and their fragrances
distinct. Leaves dancing and the sun
infinitely slowly advancing into afternoon.

Once after hours of dust-dry August hay
she closed still itching eyes to find
moonlight silvering poppies and pear tree
over flowers like fondant and the moss-soft stones
so luminous, submarine, that she
could see to stoop and pick wild strawberries.

After a sunset red with ice she knew
the garden should be frozen hard

but glimpsed warm-breathing trees
one low hedge of lavender in flower
and gold ripening at the heart of the white rose
calm in a bowl of humming summer air.

She did not want the garden to stay young
but when it last came she recognised a ruin.
Abandoned, overgrown, the delicate white flowers
had drowned and the bright shapes were blurring.
All its rooms were empty; and she woke
dull-hearted, ready for mysterious bad news.

A Cowrie Shell for Saiorse

Happy as a clam the idiom says;
Safely closed? But though her eyes
Are clear, still, as the summer sky
Reflected in the sea around her island
Each of her sixteen hundred days has been
A sort of opening. In her company
Days become mysterious again.
Waking to the whispering rush
Of rain in drought, she's almost scared:
But where's the sun gone? Why did it go?

Why? and *But* — are key words now.
Part of the program she sometimes
Resists. *Am I pretty
In this dress?* Then deliberately
Dirtying the pink, splashes mud
With a throaty chuckle. Small fluffy creatures
Work on her like a reflex: at ducklings
Bright still with albumen, she wails
O but I LIKE them... as if
It hurt, the need to hold and stroke.
The emptiness of arms, the iron gate.

The world she draws
Sitting warm in my lap, intent,
Is full of faces split with smiles
Of window-crowded houses
Where yellow vans park in gardens
Perfectly bisected by long, white paths.
They're taking the children away.

Then, a solemn bestowal
Of signed work *These are to you.*
I blutack them to the wall, with the others.

Today we search on Solfach for the lucky shells.
In pockets soft as ash and bright as salt
We dredge the detritus of separate small lives
Blended, but their colours kept distinct

For the whole one, keeping its secrets close.
Cowries are like THIS — she shows two
Fists, tight-clenched, and then looks troubled:
How can the little fish get OUT?

And while we sift and fumble in the sand
The mind relaxing so the eye can thread
Its focus, images of elsewhere, other voices,
Swarm: fragments of the chrysalis
I was; the wide-gazed woman
This little girl will turn into;
A recurring dream of lucent shadows
With the lulling slip of seawater that floods
Mosaic and marble while in a full-length
                              crimson dress
I step deliberately down, deeper in.
And last week a colleague, Bryn, at thirty-nine
Confiding hope that Dateline saves him
From loneliness. *I just haven't time.*

But Saiorse's grim. The waif who tagged along
Holds out a clutch of shells, pearl-pale
Against her thin and grubby palm.
I can't explain that Lissa needs some joy.
Her will clenched tight, she wants, she *must*
Find one. I try to cheat by slipping her
A shell found years ago, when I too might
Have wished. But she's already learned.
For luck to work it has to be self-found.

Sevens

The death of Elgar

It was six rough sailors and their boy
found him fallen where the Virgin's spring
seeps over in a flood of watermint —
an old man wrapped in deer and sealskin
gorse flowers and grass in his wild hair
self-anointed with a cross of earth.
He had planned, often, for a solitary death

with no-one left to sponge his face
to wet his lips with ale-and-water.
Without hearth-warmth to ease his flesh
needing no sacraments or bells, no speech left
to bequeath his story, he had hoped for strength
to pray one last time in his sky-charged cave.
But even now, he saw, a purpose offered.

Seven years he had safe in the nest
until, his father drowned, he must make shift
to keep his mother and the young ones fed.
Snatched out fishing by Norse raiders
seven years a kitchen slave in Ireland
then caring for another master's horses
till Rory King of Connacht saw his strength

and with daily threat of death made him
royal executioner. Fetid straw
and broken food, the casual goading
he was used to: what he could not stomach
was the boasting leading up to battle
and his part after with the captured enemies:
the crack the small bones made

between his nape-pressed thumbs; the groan
the bladed victim sank with to his knees;
the jerking dance played to its end;
the way fear-sweat dried acid and
panic or courage both set blue-white

36

in staring eyes. The hardest to forget
were those who told him they forgave him.

His speech was slow and thick; they grew
unwary. One night, the leg-iron loose,
he slipped away, slave-hounds silent at his heels,
south to where the great rocks lean
sheer down to the sea. Cliff-cunning he had,
learned as a boy sent down to gather eggs
or fat-fledged seafowl for the pot. From hand

to toe-hold under the stars' firm net
he crawled, waited for the tide to ebb
and four miles further in a cave he found
a boat with sweeps and sail. Hugging the coast
at last he reached safe harbour and took ship
for home. But winter winds shift north.
Split apart and swamped, clinging and choking

washed ashore as flotsam, he found welcome.
Seven years he shared monks' bread and offices
living as a hermit halfway between
the passion of the sea and the purity of the sky
in the cramped, dank cave where the most fervent
of confessors once loosed prayers —
not like Elgar's modest sparrow-flocks

but hugely individual, patient soaring fulmars
or persistent hawks that shook the faithful
with the wind-beat of their passing. Here, the last
of the old brothers eased into the earth
came voices, visions shimmering
like thin flame, and food sent down —
flesh brought by the birds and each third day

fish from the rock, a long, lithe-muscled eel.
Once he feasted on a princely stag
fresh-killed for the finding by the waves.

Until the last of his soul-friends told him
what to do: pray for all the faithful, dig
a fathom down between the ancient graves;
lie down and wait for death, the last long sleep.

Earth was no stranger; he had lived
years within its close embrace. And sky
was only the last sail he had to fold.
The words all stowed, it was time
to let himself go down into the net
to drown in the thundering breath
that would hold him firm and wake him

on another welcoming island, cliffs
crowded with white wings in sunlight.
At the last, they felt a hush
as in a shell, listening for a sea far-off
and round him saw a growing light
luminous, pale gold, *Like buttercups*
one said later, at his ordination.

He saw their faces changing, and rejoiced.

From the Stone

Even on this throw of rock
a hierarchy of knowing.

This old Abbey stone, in the sun
is the colour of honey, highlighting
what seems a face —
eyebrows, puckered cheeks
a gathering of wryness, or resistance
bunching, like a ganglion
waiting to be triggered.

Holub on gargoyles:
"angels, desperate
with claws and open mouths
turning white into black"

and R. S. Thomas' "furious stone face
a god gone small
and resentful"
                    but these features
glaring from Nant stable wall
sprout from no ferment on the underside
of holiness, deserve no reverence
though I have seen processions
even a touch of circus purple turn

from the tower rotting like a hollow tooth
round the honey that it hardened on
to tread nettles by the rusty water-tank;
peering, trace
the insinuations of a sneer
and draw back into speculation

while I skulk between this godlot
and the canswiggers,
skirting the esoteric urgencies
of tide- and light- and bird-watcher
of sheep and slug-gatherer

exulting merely in the sea's strong breath
its perpetual euphoria of assent
and how light loves its seven colours
letting each be itself, and other

but I too wonder how the face came from
                           the stone
for it must have been waiting
blind and patient
under wind and rain's persistent fingers
working the stone
back into sand; waiting
for the casual knife, the quarter-hour
of enforced idleness
for the boy to scrape it into focus;
waiting
to challenge recognition
and outstare the twentieth century.

From each discipline, they
— out of what they know is kindness —
embrace me and commiserate
for my lack of faith or fun

and I — out of what I am not sure —
am silent, knowing only
time goes on
scraping the dust
from the stone, and from our faces.

Encounter

Cyclopterus Lumpus, the lumpsucker:
"the male renowned for his solicitude"
says the *Observer's Book of Sea Fishes*
explaining how while the mother draws back
to deep water, he minds the nest
in the frontier territory between tides.
Locking himself to the rock below low tide
he sprays the eggs with bubbles
of sea frothy with air, week after week
as summer ripens. When the tide is out
he crouches in the shade and keeps them cool
spraying them with water stored within.
"At this time they are most vulnerable
to birds, rats, and other predators."

Picking up what pots he can, early on the tide,
the sea clear as a child's eye
skirting Ogof Morlas and the kittiwake rock
the fisherman sees something unusual floating —
lumpy black, a sack of something or a plastic bag —
floating on the ebb out from the island.

He throttles back and lets the water slow him.
The blotch resolves itself into a fish
dark, lead-blue-black
drifting, head down, apparently dead.
It's round as a plate, two handspans across.
He scoops it lightly aboard

and knows, at first touch
it is alive, but without panic or resistance;
just a quickening, an awareness
inside the spiky carapace, the old bag of its skin.

He sits it doll-like on the hauler box, upright
not flopping or floundering like any other fish
unperturbed, but adjusting

41

like an old man coming unstartled from a drowse
in his own house, or a thinker, absorbed,
leaving a library for full sun and bustle.

Despite the black leather with its seven rows
of studs, the candy-striped Mohican crest
of fin and tail, a seriousness

and on impulse, he bends his face
level to look closer
to identify, and sees the fish
swivel its eyes
to look straight back at him.

Not large like whiting or bass
staring as though they hardly believe in themselves
but serious, controlled, intelligent
returning his gaze as if it knows what it's about
fitting the man into its pattern of sense.

Perhaps it is exhaustion, dying
that frees it from fear, (how light,
how scuffed and drained of shine its skin)
or the genes' programming
to outface danger so that they survive.

Gently he lowers it to the water
and watches as slowly, purposefully
the lumpsucker sinks
deliberately down, into the dark.
The sounder here shows fifteen fathoms.

Case History

There was a boy of twelve who'd never learned
To speak. Farm-bred, he had not understood
That he was more than livestock — turned
To dogs for company, came running for his food
With cats or chickens and woke with no surprise
At owls' homecoming or stars' breath on his face.
I saw him when they brought him in. His eyes
Were clear as sunlit water, held a space
We promptly crammed with language. Beyond reach
Soft wordless songs, the colours in wet stone
He loved; grass-smell; the old humanity of touch.
His brightness died, and we began to realise
Speech wakes in us so confident, so soon
What deeper dumbnesses might it disguise?

Western Horizon

Space anchored by light
where three colours meet, glance back
and beckon us out.

Next Day

Halfway along the track, he pauses
so he will see her first. Nothing seems to move.
The haymakers have followed the last load
back to the farm for tea, and even sheep
lie humped in shade. He climbs the gate
into a cave of trees and sees but hardly feels
shadow-washing on his arms. From in here
sunlight makes the landscape look unreal,
bright and empty as a set. He can't
blend in — the rustle and the hurry of his blood
will not be cooled. The whole hot afternoon
bucks beneath him like a motorbike.

Then, she is coming, pale dress
fluttering past gaps and gateways, blinking
behind hedges. Without thought his eye
calculates her speed and course, surging his body
over the fence and up the path
to meet her. But where is she?
Slow minutes, scanning; sun's begun to lean
against his shoulder when she moves again
drifting across the field to look at flowers.

All right then. Let her come finding him
if she still wants to. Squares against the wall
monolith-still amongst the flies. He feels
but will not watch
her drawn towards him, approaching slowly
and always so obliquely
it might be just the wind that brings her.
When she is close enough to see
him looking, the dark head dips
like a blown flower, her eyes becoming busy
among tractor ruts and dried-out stones.

The wall pushes him off towards her.
There is a cool bare space
carefully between them as they walk.

When, by accident, their bare arms brush
they veer apart like startled birds
but another thread is caught, they are wound in

to the moment when her lips again
will be more welcoming than sunlight,
his more delicate than flowers.

On Retreat

She has been, she tells me, so careful
Of her children — cautious even of care,
But keeping them free from cold
And flies and hunger, responsible
About check-ups at the dentist
And quiet hours for homework.
Always, she would keep from them
The bare boards and the shouting
Of her childhood

Rejoicing that they have inherited
so little to reproach her for, no sign
Of short sight, crooked toes or asthma.
The easy gladness of their growing
Kept the cold wind from her back.
But now the girl
Weeps until her gaze is empty
As a wave in winter, starves her body
Because humanity, she screams, is rotten

And the small son
Whose earth-brown eyes were warm
With mischief or with wondering
Begins to ask why there's no cure
For cruelty. Now she must explain

The fairness that she's taught them
Is a game; not all the monsters
Can be spelled away in talking,
And being happy
Is a visitation or an accident.
She's here to work out how
To find some focus for the fear —
That the painless childhood she has shared
                                    with them
Has not cost the toughness to survive.

Myxomatosis

Once set, he had to keep on
killing rabbits that summer on the island,
a moment's sharpness in his hands
seeming kinder than three days' long dying
in that heat. But though they crouched
so openly for death
they screamed stronger than babies
and struggled like wet cats. Bucks
fought drunkenly but the very young
with no resistance in them were the worst.

He had to try to smash their pain
with sticks and stones, inexpert jabs
edge-handed, at the tender nape.
Swinging them head-down against
a wall acted out atrocity he'd glimpsed
on some old news film of Vietnam.
In the end, taught himself a trick:
blunt to the sharp, starved arch
of the backbone, the swollen, suppurating head
he felt noose-fingered for the small hot pulse
and stopped it. Each corpse

he laid carefully aside to be stripped clean.
For a few weeks, even from the sea
the island breathed a foulness
until, two days before he left,
the weather broke. Warm rain
softened the dead flesh, washing it out
with its swarming crews
leaving only scattered vertebrae
the small white cogs of suppleness
to find their new connections in the earth
or wait, numb as shells
for moonless winter nights
to smooth them out completely.
The Friday that he left, he was fourteen.

Meanwhile, in Another Part of the Island

Margiad is weeping for her daughter.

      Half-dressed on the white bed
in a room bleached as a cell
      washed with light off the water
weeps for the daughter she will never have

      letting salt trace the score-marks
of smiling, letting tears run into the perm,
      tasting the squeeze and release
from her own inner ocean.

      In the hard calm moments after
conjures the warm dimpled hand
      (her son's already angular, hard-skinned)
of a thought-child.

      It began on trains, in waiting-rooms and queues
of supermarket strangers, accepting as her due
      two children, boy and girl, so by now she tells
Gwenno's birthday easily as Geraint's.
      Never a baby; safely past that
Sometimes lately, gravely adolescent
      taller than her mother, a little deafness
keeping her shy. And once
      at home in Hafod (another winter funeral)
running in to say she'd found
      a nest of kittens in the hay, there might have been
a cake with seven candles
      on the dresser. But no singing.

In this room though, this stronger, salt-rinsed air
      it seems not comfort but a kind of madness
no denying act or grieved late loss
      can speak for. Whatever quiet depths
the fairness floats from, whatever broken shoot
      holds out this hand of blossom now
its spring is wilder, deeper in, than blood.

So, not a ghost, unless part of herself
invoked as Lalla, scapegoat, secret friend,
        had only faded in the din of school
and waited all these lifetimes to be called.

        The sun is weakening. It's time
to cheer the final minutes of the game.
        Pulling on jeans and doing up her face
she shrugs. Safer than shoplifting. Or gin.
        Imagines what Faculty wives would gloat
(hawks over stubble); how Wyn's eyes would start
                culturing a smoothness to keep her wrapped in.

But decides: no killing off with hormones.
        So, there is still
the faintest echo of a separate pulse
        in the shadowed room behind her, what might
                                have been
a footstep with hers on the stairs
        and a lightness, like a small hummed tune
she keeps on almost catching.

Stone

In the lining of his weekend anorak
he probes a lump through birds-nest fleece
and siltings of accumulated grit
from all the hills and beaches
they walked last year. Caught
between crooked forefinger and thumb
it becomes again a small clenched world
seeded in the dark, worn smooth by seas,
the halves of reconciliation healed.

He remember it a mint-white, a trophy;
but what he draws out to the light
is pock-marked, stained as if with age
or rot, a kernel shaken loose
still blind; one shining fragment
clouded over, cold. A stone to throw.

After the Storm

Far off in the dark
The old sea heaves and mutters
The mad pack outrun.

In the Hayfield

St James' Day, I was in Safeway, getting food in
When I felt — like needles — in my hands.
Sharp, deep, piercing through the palm.
I had to leave half of my shopping.

At the end of the row, we stop, lean on our rakes.
Laughter from the unloading in the rickyard
Drifts down from Plas. The rest have flopped into the
shade.

Then, at teatime on Good Friday
They began to bleed, all over the white cloth.
For six years, at three o'clock, soaking through the bandages...
Then on the Sunday, I saw Our Lady on the landing.

Her face is water-puffy, pale, her hair
Carefully set. Marks shirt and corduroys say
Safely middle-class; but she glitters and leans close.

In a vision of Bethlehem I held her baby.
He grew heavier and heavier in my arms.
I unwrapped the shawl. I saw his heart.
It was dark as liver and constantly bleeding.

From the sun-drenched rock, seals testify.
The tractor splutters in the yard; around us
There's stretching, yawns. This load will be the last.

It's been three years now. Only the nailmarks left.

She holds her hands out, the pale vulnerable palms
Towards me. Each smooth, unscarred, quite clear.
She touches three spots reverently.

At Easter, still, they itch.

51

Nocturnal

Outside, soft folds of shiny light
fall round him and he feels
another sort of creature now.
Behind the battlemented farmyard walls
the moon's a brilliant silver eye
Stars move among the clouds and on some
                    black flow
of air, pale moths are floated past him
into nowhere. *Too light for shearwaters*
his father's voice says in his head;
it is, clear as day. But odd, half-recognised —
daytime's dark twin. Like a negative,
another side to things, where animals
and birds can have their turn.

He sees the lighthouse beam go round
a giant finger probing
shadows solid as the shapes themselves
pools deep enough to drown in
but all the surfaces washed clean.

He looks up at the blinded window of the room
where they are sleeping. Once, twice, three times
it shudders with the sharp white light.
He could go in to see them sleeping
if he dare, as his mother told him
she came to tuck him up each night —
look at their secret faces, wonder where
their dreams are taking them. Or wake them up.

The grass is cold beneath his feet.
A sudden wind says something like a word.
He finds he has to whisper what he's learnt.
This world's as real as ours.
The moon's a white stone under water now.

Five stripes of brightness lie across the stairs
from the spear-shaped window in the porch.
He creeps through each, all movement slowed
fearful now of creaks and challenges
of endless dulling explanations.

I went out last night when I woke up
he begins to tell them, making islands
with his Weetabix. *Mm? That was naughty...*
turning up some talk of Parliament.
She is smiling as she scribbles postcards.

He shrugs the blinds down
on his mind's eye. But it's been seeded
with a germ of secret lunar knowledge
that even when he's old will pulse and put
                                    out shoots
unlooked-for, that he'll try to share.

Inside the Bubble

Though it was Sunday, they were shearing
Over on the island. We crossed so early
The beaches were still clean
As the tide had left them, the sea's face
Greasy with sleep, its wrinkles
All smoothed out. When *Pererin*

Had droned away behind the lighthouse
We felt stillness
Surging back; it bulged
Against our eardrums for a second
Stretching itself
To let us in. Seals were crooning on the west

But we saw nothing moving all the time
We were wading through the pastures' breath.
Deep in the blades of iris leaves
Found a moorhen's nest, empty but warm,
And looked to count how many sheep
Had made it this time to the mountain

But there was only quartzglint and the bracken
Flowing through the crevices like lava
Swirling in slow motion round the rocks.
The houses sat so purposefully still
I felt we might just catch them whispering
Or changing pose. A drift of words

Too blurred to catch the tune of language
Floated like the smell of flowers
Over Plas front garden wall.
We too kept voices low.

Then, *Listen.* Held between the generator's thump
And the bell for morning service
Dripping its polite reminder
Into the pooled air. *We ought to go —*

Which way? To busy talk and friends
And rolling fleeces? Or to sing among the stones?
Like a wily ewe, I led my lamb
Through a gap in the mountain wall

And all morning we truanted
In a simmering haze, buoyed up
As if by faith or summer ocean
Threading high paths an instep wide
Between the scratchy gold of gorse

Sprawling whenever we felt weary
On rabbit-lawns or like the birds
Under roofs of just-uncurling bracken
Where earth breathed herbs and faint warm honey.

It makes me feel faded
The boy said, and while perhaps he only meant
Quiet, or heat, or some thought half-prised open
The words fitted. Space and light hummed on
But time was loosened round us
Shimmering without that rise and dip

Of personal horizons.
Then, pots all lifted, tangle-nets hauled in,
The boat was waiting down in Solfach
And suddenly we had to run and leap and scramble
Through rock-pools (filling up so quickly)
Churning the smoothness, having to wade out.

Broc Môr
for P.H.J.

Mornings, still, the islanders "walk round",
working the shore for a first finding
for what high tide has left.
Once, ranked on the rocks hours-long
they'd wait or post their kids to watch
to make sure of a cask or solid plank.
In rivalry or spite sometimes they'd wade
or, boots and all, leap wide into the swell.
Dim, the Frenchman's sheepdog, did a sea-fetch
trained to nose good pickings safe ashore.

The sea provided: a barrel bursting with butter
sweating salt; sea-moulded lumps
of dark wax I still polish with; the captain's chair
at the head of our table; wrecked and waterlogged
the boat called *Benlli* homing in on echoes
to wait off Caswennan; the Japanese mask
that hung by the fire to send Tŷ Pella kids
shrieking to bed; Arthur's clogs, the left
picked up in March, its match two months later.
Once in the Narrows a whole ash tree
trunk wide as a table, riddled with shipworm,
generations of voyagers. In wartime
grey barrels bobbing in like schools of whales
found full of still-sweet water. And a real whale
mine-mutilated, stinking in Traeth Ffynnon.

Survey in Henllwyn, 1984:
0.1% was pinecones, plant seeds, nuts.
Three thousand and sixty plastic items
thrown up in three weeks on this shore
with clothes pegs, sweet wrappers, pencils, string.
One sandwich, intact (corned beef and tomato).
Beercans, and the jellyfish-clear slings
from fourpacks. Light bulbs. Galaxies of condom rings.
A bottle of Valium with the name washed blank.

We read the labels and the languages:
Brazil, Chile, Finnish, Afrikaans.
Coal sacks from Arklow, milk bottles
out of Drogheda. Santiago tonic
and a University of Miami driftmarker
four years crossing, Bahamas to Bardsey.

These summers when I walk the shore
it's scattered with bottles sealed on names.
I uncork a breath of sun-warmed oranges:
Hi, this is Sharon from Merseyside.
On a day trip to Douglas.
A boy in Wicklow wants a penpal.

To seal your name inside a bottle
toss it to the wider-spreading waters
seems like offering bait, to trawl for a reflection
as a cave might sniff out ears with echoes.
For what's a name except an echo
of echoes marrying between two minds?
The bright green bud from whose heart
filaments of self may be unfurled —
Shane or Cynddylan, Marilyn, Nuala of the Free
or victim Hester... And Voyager,
our name drifting in the cosmic tide:
Is there anybody out there?

What readers on the future's
littered shore? Deep ocean is
a kind of archive: random fragments
of whatever we have lost or thrown away
dry in the wind, catch the light, and testify.

Brenda and the Golden Snake

I

Orpheus obsessed her, though it was
  trees and streams that plucked the air
for her. She woke the whiteness of the page:
  rocks opened their dumb mouths
and the sea's horizon danced.
  Seals swam in the wake of her singing.

But she was also the lost one
  the seeker after sunlight
Eurydice, follower, falling back
  into the zero of her own cry.

Sunlight was where she belonged.
  In a house with no dark corners
hers was the only shadow.

  Child in a garden bounded by slates
jagged grave markers jabbed in upright
  she taught herself colour
drawing on their dullness
  with shatterings of stone, tracing
a pattern, a swirl of bright scratches.

  Strong links are not broken.
I believe in never and always and only.

II

  Like a child, blankness
threatened her: she sang,
  conjuring melody to feed the echoes
scarfed dullness with brilliance and in the rock
  shaped mouths like openings to safety;
named nine colours
  in the fur of the trapped hare
then sought an island
  treasures from the sea
and a fiction of herself

58

in a small boat alone
waking to grey water and the curious gaze
of seal-people (gentler these
than the human figures, watching
with closed faces, hardened,
used to narrowing their eyes
against intruders or the sun
not betrayed by pain, or dazzled.
With their stiff black hair
cat-faced, secretive, remote as Pharaohs).

On the beach where the boats are loaded
rocks split open show
the primaeval passage of a worm
before this earth-crust hardened.
She held time in a stone within her hand
fitted her finger to that ancestral groove.

She had other tunnels to explore.
Always tempted by the dark, the swirling,
she knelt to peer through ice
polished by the moon, and on a winter
mountain
with her pony, waved defiance
at drones of bombers on their way
to destroy Liverpool. Sketched melting
snow-memories of wings and hungered
to dissolve to a small brown seed
blowing bright-starred
new summer after summer
in the wind-stirred land.

III

From both islands that she found
she watched the sea break colour
from the grey, feeding her heart
on its bright flux. As midnight drew
the faintest rim of zodiacal light

down over the horizon
she said a valediction for each day
danced under.

The only place for me to live!

But she began to dream of embarkation:
white ships, high-prowed with
Breton sailors, big-thighed, swaggering.
Petra and Luxor, the light-clusters
of cities. Then fled the winters
hurrying south to heat and clarity
breezes warm with herbs and woodsmoke
garlic, wine, and kinder seas.

No sanctuary of the mind:
the framework of escape had closed her in.
She knew a shut-in hunger to be bodiless
travelling through obsessions
towards the someplace that might prove itself
a porch of infinity.

Every voyage at the end is cruel.

IV

She remembered Orpheus again
by the cold blue sea that washed her dreams
On Enlli, where the rocks at last
had closed their ranks against her.
Once curled seductively as dolphins
or opening wide porches
her paint began to shape them
pierced, blinded, broken conch shells.

The fish with the knowing eye
poised at the heart of the sharp-edged pool
winks with connivance.
Orifices gape to a wound-red ocean.
Boats lie beached like whales

the baleen striations of their clinker sides
waiting to be butchered.

All that matters is the voyage.

The pictures fragment into totems
        a mosaic of eyes
defiantly bright, litanies
            where shapes cluster like an Indian blanket
gasps of paint and incantations
          eyes and gaping mouths —

Every voyage at the end is cruel.

        Those last years, back inland,
blindly she tried to root
        but, exhausted
let a long misery of winter
          blur her distinctness;
it sucked her down.

        At the end, she knew
she was both — the singer
          face turned always to the sun
and woman bitten by the golden snake
          strong enough to try
to deliver herself from the dark.

        Eurydice
unglueing her eyelids
          dragging herself back up
but the heavy shoulders turning
          the ash of knowledge
rising in her throat.

It sucked her down
          like a blown seed, like a shape
in the melted snow, a gasp
          the ocean heals itself around.

Fragments of her voyage go on singing.

At the End of Summer

It was easy, looking over towards Ireland
      To understand the myth of Avalon.
At our backs the colours of endurance
      The Sound brusque, a military blue, but
West — translucent, milky-pale, vermilion —
      The ebb-tide sliding into place like syrup.

Walking on the headland after hearing
      Muggeridge on the radio, at eighty
Welcoming the thought of death, we watched
      The slow sun settling for the night
And a fish-scale moon hauled up as smoothly
      To drip silently above the lighthouse.

Grass was rasping, bracken shrinking back.
      It was time for the flocking of birds.
Below us on the cliff the nests were empty
      The storm-petrel's cleft gone dumb.
But the year's warmth lingered as if all took breath
      Before the slow movement began.

The long arm of the mainland down to Aber
      Was shadow-pleated and against the hills
Small gibberish of stars was signalling.
      I could blot it all out with one finger
While we seemed effortlessly floating outward
      Towards the shining, that mesmeric edge.

We stood close together, facing out.
      I could not guess where his thoughts lay.
Perhaps as well. Our own myths fade
      Slower, more tenderly that way.

Watchers

All day this western shore is being watched
as though it is a frontier or a screen.
Since noon, the tide's signalling lenses
have been promising to turn
and return, light drawing our gaze
to share in its dance, show flesh too
can shine. Seals swim smooth
as though calm itself could be beguiled;
quiescent gulls and oystercatchers
drag shadow-moorings. The whole long
                              weathered coast
lies back and lets salt cool its wounds.

A Wil sky, Ingrid calls it, pointing
where cloud seas and islands beckon
liquid gold, where silver archipelagoes
promise strange voyaging
You can almost see him, fishing from the Aron.
Ten years since his death, and still it's strange
coming back and finding he's not here.

Earth tilts to evening. From here we see
Tŷ Pella kitchen window wink, as if like us
it waits to catch that rumoured brilliance
the rare green flash
of day's wings, disappearing

but our faces stream with only ordinary light
watching the apparently effortless
ships drawn across the western rim
on strings of soundwaves, telexes,
printouts of schedules, cargoes, profits
that tide of paper and preoccupations
we prefer to keep below the glisten,
seeing only bright masts or a silhouette
the grace of voyaging
in sunlight that's already
passing over, leaving us, beyond.

63

Douglas

You can see his profile
Strong as Socrates (but not thick-lipped)
Massive with dignity on stamp or coin:
But a man of whim, of humour and caprice.

His steep green-shimmering garden
Echoes the exuberance of his mind:
Contorted forms, extravagance
And the chuckling company of running water.
His house is crammed with gadgets.

All day on the island he shores up
Invents small intricate devices
To gauge the shifting of the earth
And talks of dying
As someone else would plan a journey.

He works alone, or like Prospero
Directs minions with his staff
Towards a vision of more permanence
Thick hair bleached by years, blue eyes
Clear as a navigator's,
He is moonstone or malachite, incorruptible.

I walked with him once along a broken shore
Where great slabs, like the front of churches
Split, were thrown down,
Rubble that seemed still cooling
Round a block like a vast stone coffin
Wet-dark, inscribed by weather.

That night I dreamed him with three women
In a circle of silver
Black figures, black boat beached in a
Circle of silver.
Around us was a dark eye, darkening.
His white hair gleamed like alabaster
As he picked a way along the shore
To the darker sills he must discover
And find a way over, alone.

Keeping in Touch

This is Viv, in Milton Keynes...

I always think of her against the shining
west, her eyes the sweet clear green
of goosegogs not yet fully ripe —
green with the force of light behind.

Easy to imagine them at moonrise
turning emerald and luminous.
She is topaz and amber
earth quickened by fire

but drawn back always to cold shores
where light brings out the shades
in rocks and people, and confirms
that all shades fit.

This island won her with its fullness
a seamless ripening that took her in
and whispered here might be the place
for the bright strands to converge

Perhaps it was the way
rock cupped water for her
in limestone palms, the primroses
waited to be found

above the gull screams on the northeast corner
the velvet stillness of the evening fields
or vast sky filling to infinity
with brilliant dust

Riding the white mare above the booming caves
aware of living at the edge of knowing
what tides of sea or sky
would leave within her reach tomorrow

Not fighting it but sinking in
she told me, sensing she must be on passage;
that there was something in her, even here
not ready yet to be contained

that is still waiting
poised as it were in a dry cave
looking out over a valley
waiting for a focus to gather itself.

Under the woodruff skin, the contours
she has schooled to gentleness, her bones
have a predator's edge.
She steps delicately, lifted face

alert as frost. Even her hands
seem to listen. From the teeming starlessness
of Milton Keynes, she posts off letters, phones:
nurses her hunger, promises herself

she'll keep in touch.

Storm

Deepening low, two hundred miles south-west of Rockall...

And, yes, the sky was feathered
for the coming wind, the bay at Solfach full
of smashed kelp, warm and gastric-smelling;
murk building on the horizon
and sea's smooth skin crawling
remembering storms, sweating messages
in beery scum to warn the shore.
Soon the waves will let go, run,
risk all together
while land dwellers grip, rooted, desperate.

A big swell blooms slowly like a sigh
to swish long tunnels in the cliff under our feet.
The old bull seal in the lee of the Gaswallt
breaks the uneasy quiet, snorting air.
Two ewes graze yards from the heave and shift
of the waiting-to-be-herded waves.

Three days of storm and lurching seas
roar like a distant rodeo, there's
the constant hiss and plunge and after-shock
of staggered detonations. Waves
curl, buck, and rear, come crashing down
in a flurry of white froth. Maen Iau
shows its teeth between dark lips. Each skerry swings
in the loop of a bolas, whirled by the tide.

Behind blown cumulus the sun pale and helpless
shows a cyclops eye
weeping and flayed. Close-hauled,
wings have to whip and ply
to shudder through the beating seas
of air. Even we can hardly
push our bodies through
the black and silver steel of showers
to borrow coffee, beg cigarettes

declare the world well lost — who cares
about the job, the kids' new school, that flight
to San Francisco booked for Tuesday — delay,
a few days more, we laugh, is what we wanted.
Before at last getting to the point:
a couple of urgent calls on the R.T.

Through the Weather Window

We wake in luminous quiet
a sky all fawning silk and silver.
Snails, fat wall fruit, creep and chuckle.
The four-year-old squats at *pictures of the sky —*
slower than television in the lane puddles.
The sea has a leery stare.

The forecast's bad again, farewells snatched.
A hell of a swell — we'll make a run for it.
Cross before the flood comes.

The boat rolls, and dips, and rises
as the ocean's grey skin heaves.
Green troughs yawn, folded ventricles
sliced to the aortic quick
to the mineral veins
of cobalt, emerald and viridian
running fast, nudged over
to pulse and burst again.

If the engine cut, we would be carried
backwards by the heave and kick, the
                                        bunching muscle
of the current. Each crest
is an emancipation.

Mid-Sound, the pattern breaks
to a confused sea, random rearings;
sudden, spiteful spray and one huge heave
as if the kraken, gnarled and pressure-blind,
chose suddenly to stir. At our back, stormclouds
already massing and a solemn Scotsman on the VHF
calls *All ships* with warnings, *imminent.*

There is a moment, sudden as
slack water, when the island's pull
falls away. Between one wave-lurch

and the next, your gaze is drawn
to where the mainland stretches out warm fingers.
Summer pastures beckon.

The wake's a long furrow
that shines with all our stories.
Some of us look back, but the island
has already turned away, become horizon.

Llŷn

Skies tower here, and we are small.

Winters, we sleep on a flap of land
in a dark throat. We taste the salt
of its swallow. Huge cold breaths
hurtle over, cascade down
till we feel the house hunch.

Along the northern edge, the rocks
go on holding on
but taught obedience by ice, the clays
of the southern shore slide palely under.

When morning comes at last
houses sit up with pricked ears
on reefs of land the black tide
leaves, or sidle crab-wise
to the lane, their small squashed faces
giving nothing of their thoughts away.

In summer, flowers loosening with seed
reach out to fingerstroke
cars passing in the long sweet dusk.
Hay-meadows sigh. Pearl-pale
in the bracken on the headland
shorn ewes step delicate
and wary as young unicorns.

The sea we look out over is a navel
the wrinkled belly-button
of an older world: after dark
like busy star-systems, the lights
of Harlech, Aberystwyth, Abergwaun
wink and beckon. The sun's gone down
red as a wound behind Wicklow.
A creaking of sail away
Cernyw and Llydaw wait.

Once, here was where what mattered
happened. A small place
at the foot of cliffs of falling light;
horizons that look empty.
If we let ourselves believe it,
fringes.

Island of Dark Horses

Each thought, each step
was barefoot across lava.
Silence, bruised, brimmed in their wake.
Those who saw them pass by night
claimed they lit the darkness   5
with cold fire; that sapphires
and ruby, crystal haloes,
shimmered round them as they walked
but there were jewels only
in the furnace of their minds   10
where Christ's words
glowed, their colours melting
and reshaping softer.

After the burning
of Benlli's city, they were marked men,   15
Garmon and his brothers.
Men moved aside for them.
Mothers hid their babies' faces.

None could shut out the cries,
the roar of flame and the smell of fat.   20
So he led them north, seeking cleansing
from the power he had loosed
through penance on that cold island
the foreign tyrant's stronghold
whose fighting men were all called home   25
or sailed to the struggle with Cadell.

At last they reached the rocky place
where land looks out before it drowns
to the whaleback island waiting
against sunset. As dusk thickened   30
the wind dropped, winter wave-swell
fell away and a strange light
grew and strengthened on the ocean,
a phosphor glow unlike the moon
that turned to mist and curdled   35

low on the water. They paddled out
through rafts of silent birds.

Two nights later, fire was seen
soon after nightfall, and in summer,
to the lowbrowed shelters on the hill   40
came other men of faith and power —
Tanwg, Maelrhys, Hywyn, Cadfan —
and it was turned to Insula Sanctorum.

Lauds

First thing, the sky is rinsed and pearly flesh
inside a shell where white horizons   45
unclench slowly. Moths swim in grey air
above a seabed of grey heather.
Burdened by what will be brightness
the thin grass between the bracken's strung
with trawls and filaments,   50
small basins of thread, fine as smoke,
that will dry to a glisten, to the invisible shadow
of caves where hunger waits.

Who hears the first voice, breaking the skin
of the small hours' silence? Already gull   55
and kittiwake provide a consonance
for the jargoning of skylark, blackbird, thrush.
When the blue of the full day breaks
innocent of the names and offices we give them
(surf in an ocean of light) our hours   60
quicken, rouse and gather to roll in
to spend themselves easily as waves.

At sun's first touch on the east side
Kim rolls from her sleeping bag, reaching
for binoculars, sketchpad. Too late.   65

The tiercel startles in a scatter
of white feathers from a ledge
in the steep green sweep where a shearwater
lies on its back like a sacrifice.
Hand and eye lock on as he circles   70
swoops *like an arrow with closed wings*
to land, and swing the blade of his gaze
towards her, calmly, as she might study
a fish sealed in its sphere, in glass or ice.
Settled back to the plucking, beak begins   75
to scythe, snipping bone like pliered wire.
The female on the nest still makes no sound.

Nine oystercatchers, three groups of three
fly past, printed on the sky's pigeon-breast
like a logo, even their cries symmetrical.   80
Seen close, they have fanatics' eyes
those orange beaks surgical as steel.
There's a mint-bright smugness
about the morning lighthouse, its
complacent daytime wink. Roof-slates   85
gleam with the bloom of ripening plums.

Andros, Pliny called it; *Edri*
to ancient Greek mapdrawers of the western edge.
A world of waves and pouring air
the lighthouse's long steady stroke   90
in the flux of the sea.
An island where so many came to die.
Fragment of land, and a whole place, peopled,
generous with truths between the tide's
twin ceremonies of dark and light.   95

Lleuddad's covenant with the Angel of Death
is recorded in the Book of Llandâf:

No reptile shall be seen in this island
save the harmless water lizard.

The spring below the limestone crag
in the driest season shall run sweet

and those that live holy here
shall die only in succession
the oldest going first
like a shock of corn ripe for the sickle

with hands and feet unfailing
as if sleep had come upon him.
Even should any of the pure in heart
die by the way, they shall not be damned.

Thus warned, let him who is eldest prepare
not knowing at what hour
he will hear sea's long low whisper change
or feel the dark wind lapping at his feet.

Nameless graves lined with white stone
no more than two feet from each other
shall brim like wells and testaments
though only ravens witness, surf exults.

There are holds in the rock, but too small;
echoes but no answers.
Dry sand trickles through the fingers
and only our own prints follow.

Prime

Stiff breeze from the west about seven
brisks up a military blue
and clenches the bay into ruffles.
In a fern and foxglove forest,
on a cliff ringing with kittiwake calls,
on a long cross scratched into a stone
(used ten centuries later as a lintel

for a barn that's Rachel's kitchen now)
on the grazing mares picketed by foals   130
light moves in a silent tide, sharpening
the focus, letting difference shine.

Within the green walls of his garden
Arthur moves among the quiet bean flowers
picking caterpillars off cabbage plants   135
one by one, the huge striped cat
stoled on his shoulders warm, purring.
He notes the sorrel's ready for a picking.

Hermits, servants only of God, they shared
forgiveness from the heart for everyone   140
unflagging prayer for those that trouble thee
fervour in singing the office as if
each faithful dead were a true friend.
Three labours in each day: as well as prayer
work for the mind   145
reading, copying the scriptures, teaching,
and work for the hands, clearing gardens
and tending growth; gathering
what was sent for body's sustenance
fruit of sea or land, gorse for the fire;   150
brewing, baking, mending, manning
leaky skin and wicker boats; healing the sick
and brothers hurt escaping the Saxon.

Further than the diving gannets, so far
it is only a flash of perspex in the sun   155
silent as a star, a single boat
nuzzles the tide, waiting for the lift of pots
from thirty fathoms. Gulls work its furrow.
The fisherman's arms are thick with hairs
white as salt against strong, brown-speckled skin   160
his palms plated with callous
to grip the mackerel's striped-metal sides,
ink-black lobsters with their clacking tails

(boxers blundering in giant gloves).

In rooms swept bare as the seabed 16
so full of light it is company
we eat and sleep heavily
folded together like echoes.
Cried awake early, to the smell and gleam of water
we rise brimming with energy 17
hidden except to satellites
and the planes that swoop over
the play targets of our houses.

Cells of brush and turf give way
to wood and stone. Habitation, oratorium, hospice, 17
cemetery.

The cross is inscribed. On its shaft a hermit
his tunic of coarse wool-cloth to the shin
prays with bare head and uplifted arms
palms high and outward, opening the heart 18
in the old true way. It takes
three brothers to tilt it into place
above the grave. Now his name will travel,
live as long as stone endures.

Where does it begin, this sense of *home* — 18
territory, merely; space round a grave;
a people sharing concerns, the same tongue?
But languages sit lightly here or settle
briefly: pre-Celtic of the flint-droppers
in Bau Nant and Carreg marshes; warrior Gangani 19
of the Irish tribe Ptolemy first named
the promontory for; a thousand years
of monks' Latin that re-echoes in the litany
of scientists' named species. Raiders' Norse
but scarce one breath of Saxon till the lighthouse 19
sweeping the night skies four times a minute
changed the focus, pointing out. Making a haven

a trough in the rock that brought
a hundred years' prosperity. And attracting
birds of passage, eager or exhausted strangers.   200

In the shell sand the many-coloured fragments
tossed up here for a time
rub against each other, silent, still evolving.

Terce

The little church is empty. By the sundial
The great upright slab with its stone finger   205
that marks the day's four tides, the hours of prayer
(the gnomon's shadow showing third hour after sunrise)
Elgar speaks to Caradoc the master.
He is thin and threadbare, his voice uncertain.
Under a beakful of black syllables   210
dropped by a raven, he says he has been
seven years alone as the dead saints bade him
looking west to where the sun dies.

So close green flashes from its tail, a magpie
bobs and bounces   215
in long grass beside Tŷ Pella well. Stones
scoured by centuries of water
shape mossy lips where clear brims over.
Three backcombed longlashed filly foals mince near
nudging each other closer to my buckets,   220
then flounce away with nervous giggling squeals.

Willow warblers are ounces of energy and feathers
in the garden tree where the wind is strained
to a whisper, entranced by the dappling

as if there is something here   225
working for quiet
that if we stand still enough might take root....

Low down on the lichened rocks in Bau Nant
Sister murmurs her office. *For lo*
nothing in me is still, all is   23
motion, restless, everything must change...
She sits with both hands cupped open
absorbed in the rightness
of ebb and flow, sealed in a pattern
she feels as presence. *Except*   23
a corn of wheat fall to the ground
and die, it abideth alone.

The sea grunts an antiphon.
Through the crystals setting in her eyes
she sees its glitter tarnishing   24
under thunderclouds, a shadow as of
vast approaching wings. *Like rain unto a fleece*
the Lord shall come down. Laughter
floats from a high green hollow:
outside the cave where Elgar went to ground   24
to wake his visions the twins are trying
foxglove fingers, popping them in each others' faces.
Weighed down with sand eels, razorbills
pant home, weary as late-shopping wives.

Only a bubble of consciousness divides us.   25

Susan's dreaming up an island produce show
for the Observatory: best-dressed beercan,
cakes and veg and children's driftwood sculptures.
In Tŷ Pella kitchen over coffee
Lucy plans a ride across Mongolia.   25

This is a real place, small enough
to see whole, big enough to lose
our own importance. Brings us back
to our senses. Here we dig and sow and gather
walk and swim and watch birth, blossoming   26
and rot, and take ten minutes pressing

stretching, kneading bread
till something living starts to breathe and grow.
Even what we read vibrates with messages.

A tiny community of individuals   265
thrown together as on a voyage —
contained, held steady on this rock
in a time out of time, without mirrors,
freed from seeing ourselves reflected
except as close-ups in each other's eyes   270
so shadows of all the others we have been
sidle close and we begin to glimpse
what dark horses we are carried by.

Sext

By noon the colours are already tired.
Horizons squirm in the heat.   275
All's glazed. Even the sea drools
in the slack of the tide, air
is stale from off the land, lungfuls
of the Sahel. Nothing glistens
save the splashed whorled-grain   280
of pebbles, incubating abandoned
in their vast stone nests
and the shine of the maggots' dance,
the secret-feasting flies.
In the spring below Dynogoch, the eel   285
twists deeper. Insects tick away the afternoon.

A summer ceremonial procession:
Dyfrig, whom water could not swallow
fire could not eat, "Enlli's chief protector"
is scooped from his narrow bed   290
among the most holy celibates
to honour the foundation at Llandâf.
But first, Elgar, who lies shallowly so close

on the flat white stones that line the grave
must be disturbed. At spade's first touch
as if remembering a lifetime of awakenings
the white jaw opens in a smile of welcome
and seven holy teeth are shed
to be harvested and saved as relics.

Now sea speaks with the only real authority
despite tin crowns and doctorates.
The day hinges on high water.
Listen for its heave and shift
the tide swinging us all back and forth
tenderly sluttish, dragging the moon
like its child on long reins. Knuckles and spines
prickle with airbubbles
before they go under its flexing muscle.

Water has its own runes, sly perspectives:
close to shore, sand is netted
in flashing meshes of sunlight.
Deeper, green darkens; soft purple stains
like old bruises where the *Supply* gasped
and went down under thunder that night when
the swell darkened and whitened, screaming
rose a pitch higher than the wind
and a daughter's long black hair
floated like weed an armslength out of reach.

Far out light floats as on a mirror.
Close to the boat, fathomless green;
we gaze down through the seaweed forests
and acres of bladderwrack like standing corn.
Beyond, the alchemy of light and distance
turns depth a deceptive silky blue.

Crusted with anemones and barnacles
spars and masts pearly with trapped air
like pantomime regalia, guessed-at wrecks

twitch and flicker. Off the west, a German submarine
carries its seventy-year-sealed crew
to dissolution. Also grow and wait   330
the thousand scavengers of the kelp forests:
the cuttlefish that spreads its skirts
demurely over its victim; starfish,
inexorably searching. And coral,
those skeletons that look like flowers.   335
Wood from the sea, broc môr,
spits blue as it burns, spiteful with salt.

In the chapel, too young for ghosts,
where the light is thick like amber
nothing moves but the sporadic tick   340
of butterfly wings against a window.
Its red and black already fading.

Outside, there is the tap of ancient work
as Dic the stonemason repairs
a hundred years' loosening and decay   345
on the castellated walls. Hour after hour
he matches, lifts and lets each own-shaped stone
find its place and settle there.

August 1284: the House of St. Mary of Bardsey
honoured by Edward the King, fresh from feast   350
and jousting in Nefyn. He nods over the plans
— chancel, choir, refectory with dormitory
over. And a belltower. He grants ten marks
and a promise of timber. Fat voices swell
among the sprouting sandstone walls, the scent   355
of fresh-sawn wood, but stonesmith and carpenter
mutter as they're herded, early, back to work.

Through the full day's glare
in a burrow no longer than a boy's arm
the shearwater waits for night   360
held by the warmth of her silent egg.

83

None

Now the welcoming cross stands high
beckons to the waiting pilgrims
across two miles of enigmatic ocean.
And trade is good — fells of lambs and coneys   3
for Irish tweed and linen cloth,
pollack and salt herring for galingale and spices.
A gallon of every man's first brewing
mead or beer with two buckets of flour
one of oats from each homestead   3
and a good fat hen or flank of the pig.

From a high perch on the pigsty roof, Meg
scans the sea towards Wicklow, watching for dolphins.

In a cave of ferny heat behind Tŷ Capel
where they've been counting thyme and *galium* species   3
Leo makes Elaine mysterious
with fuchsia earrings. The air between them quivers.
They lie down among the flowers they have named.

On an island there is no isolation:
in a web of mutual dependence, privacy   38
is an illusion. No folly here
not guessed at, no remark
that fails to ripple in retelling.
Resentments bubble; petty jealousies
root in introspection. We gorge   38
on speculation, grow shrill
at self-importance; but move towards each other
wearing a reserve of generalities
(weather and boats, birds and sheep)
that shape a language where we can meet: 39
sharpening the focus slowly,
letting difference shine.

Tormentil for worms, thyme for the blood
self-heal for fever folded in a packet
for the armpit, where the blood   39

runs close and quick. Steep water mint
for sadness. Root of elecampane
the elfwort from the ancient gardens
Lleuddad planted, sliced, in honey,
helps all diseases of the chest and lungs   400
stays the plague itself, God willing.

Ruled by faith for a thousand years
the island's anger and acid is all old.
Thirteen centuries smoothed dry as loam
can hold in place the passions that we bring —   405
the smell of fear, its sad or gaudy fictions.
From seal and bird and human, the air here
rings with warning or desire.

Three stone crosses remind us that our days
are a mere continuance of changing light.   410
Present and past and eternity meet
in the cross enclosed in an older circle.

In Traeth Ffynnon, the rocks twist
as caught in fire, at low tide fill dark red
with weed from the deep, *gigotina.*   415
Where waves break less hard
cup coral, delicate as petals, and the dulse
the ewes tap down to graze.

Colours of the just-caught wrasse:
copper-bronze, green, orange, lapis lazuli.   420
It has jade lips, but too many small bones;
we eat it once for each triumphant fisher-child.

Seals with faces of grave elders
splash and snort, incongruously skittish.
In June calm, swarms of jelly-fish   425
drift in the Cafn, pulsing slowly
like gas mantles, translucent

parachutes of intelligence. The pool
on Maen Du is a garden of spring-forest green
its anemones sucked shiny, red sweets in a jar.   43

Each surge falls back with a shuddering sigh
leaving sand at the tide's edge moulded
like a meaning smoothed by hands.

Vespers

The pulse of this place: weather, wings
the stumbling, persistent hum   43.
of bees in late-flowering heather
and plainsong, pacing footsteps;
it is the swish, the shiver and fall
of the swathe to the scythe,
the dry stutter of tractors   44(
and the white mare's hourlong tramp
round the *dyrnwr*, the thwock and splash
of butter coming; chapel bell
and foghorn
and the shipping forecast   44!
three times a day; diesel-throb that turns
light held level in its bath of mercury;
the swing of waves and the surge and tick
of young in the womb,
the push of men and the trudge of women   45(
carrying milk, carrying water, carrying wood
                                    and children
born and unborn.

Nellie gathering her washing from the gorse
behind the school hoods a hand over her eyes
to scan the south-west
for tomorrow's weather. For the sixtieth year   45!
she calculates the springs' slow drying,
the readiness of hay, what men or boys

are still at sea, though there is no-one now
she has to keep the kettle hot for. She remembers   460
out at five to help Wil push the *Gwen,*
elvers wriggling between her toes,
the child dancing on the limekiln in her nightie
when she got back; walking with her
to find the cows (if only they would stand   465
for milking), carrying the skim
to the calves in Plas, water to the bull,
boiled potatoes to the styed pig. Running
to chase the cats from crocks of ripening cream.
Churning. Baking. Scrubbing and washing and   470
                      mending
food on the table five times a day
and in the evening, steps in the yard
click of the latch and a lighthouse keeper
for company till his watch at midnight.

On the mountain, foxgloves   475
sway on their eccentric gantries
and the carline thistle's tiny Aztec suns
dry to silver, surviving
to spike a careless hand with summer.

Day after day last August   480
I watched a chrysalis beneath our window.
I'd seen the small barred caterpillar hunch
up the wall, and found the thing like a bit
of blown leaf, a grey twist hanging there.
It filled imperceptibly   485
as fruit. Then it was twitching
like a thought, waking irritated, wriggling.
I did not see it hatch or dry its wings.

Perched on the island's spine, with field glasses
Carolyn looks south but is not seeing   490
Arthur hitching up the mower in the hayfield

or choughs that preach the free church of the air.
She is missing her daughters and fretting for
the album in a ransacked flat in Kuwait City —
pictures of the girls as babies, picnics
above the tree line in the Himalaya, faces of friends
forever now a world away. And wondering
how she will pick up the reins, where to point
the plot of her life.

This wide horizon constantly reminds us
we are all at sea, withdrawn;
larvae of ourselves suspended
ghosts of our own futures
that move towards us like drifting clouds
filling the mind with mist or startling
with sudden sculptured decision.
Some of us perhaps were refugees
or waiting to float free
but we all go back, remembering
this place and time, our bonded fellow travellers
as background, or a break, or a wise dream;
gathering images to pile up round us
as if they'd work like walls in winter.

In the hayloft he has made a bower
of exotic junk (seal's teeth strung
as necklaces, bright stones and bones and shells)
Prof hunches over latest statistics
for pitfall and sweepnet catches. *I have*
he writes, *an inordinate fondness*
for beetles. They comprise thirty percent
of all known species. He reaches for the glass
(vermouth's all gone) and, sliding down
seas of his mind's making, replays
surfing the Sound on a single wave
in a boat moonlit to a chariot of silver....

A raven croaks and rises from the crag
where the women used to watch
the island boat, their menfolk going and returning.
Fulmars surf the air, stiff-winged.
While we sit here, the world can change.   530
The raven sneers and chuckles, and wheeling high
towards mainland fields, choughs scream:
we must not let these clarities
crystalise into the one place
rooted at the centre of the world   535
lest we make exiles of our mainland selves,
turn dry husks spinning in the web
nostalgia weaves and uses
to suck us into blurring.

Scoop-shapes in the mountain slope   540
show the shape of the wind's fingernails.

Round the back, the three paths narrow;
waves wink and beckon: each deck
of this tilting ship has its own catwalk,
its companionway above the water.   545

Henllwyn: old grove, copse drowned perhaps
in the melting of the glacier that pushed
together this muddle of rock we call Enlli,
this single coherent spot
in the slow crawl of mountains   550
where we seem not so much to live as to be
lived in, moved by wind and sea and moving clouds
all the bright enigmas of our world.

King's men swing ashore with oaths and axes.
The brothers who have stayed to witness   555
watch calmly. The last of the gold
the silver pyx and reliquary
are safe in the earth by the spring
in the rock near the Abbot's House.

They have rehearsed the rote of older raids
and returns, and vowed no flinching
when the smashing starts.

Moorhen run between the brandished blades
of iris as the peregrine moth flutters by.
Seals grunt and mutter and exult, a congregation
getting the *hwyl*, with the cries
of gulls and lambs and Cristin children
playing in the hour before they sleep.

It holds the sea in the crook of its arm
this island, blending and letting
difference shine: the gaudy barber's pole
of the lighthouse, the Sea-Truck's bird-yellow
beckoning the eye to the *Storws* roof
lichened like an old tree-trunk.
For generations, its door has been shut
when all the boats are safely home.
Inside, old rope hibernates in lazy coils.

By the limekiln, you might overhear
the drifting ghost of a tin whistle tune.

A single heron hunches stealthily
where water, mirror-calm, throws back
a band of lighthouse red across the bay.

Compline

As shadows sprinkle chill and rockpools turn
to platinum and silver, quartz on the mountain
winks like Tŷ Gwydryn with its treasures.
Evening is a deepening blue silence.

Rocks and buildings pull their colours close.
Small moths flutter from the heather.

Seaward windows smoulder and the earth
breathes warmth. At last, light glides   590
back to the sea, hushing it with silent wings.
The prisms of the lighthouse blossom.
The full moon floats from its dark well.

The waxy light and heat of burning oil
the caper of the candle flame   595
wake forgiveness in the shadows,
deepen talk over cards, homebrew, or Scrabble.
Radios drift through the frequencies
with a soft hiss like the sea's.
Where skulls once piled in cartloads   600
like potatoes, the generator's thump
means Gwydion's settled to the t.v. news.

On another summer evening I remember
Gwen excited by the fossil record
names can offer; walking the maps   605
with Wil, patiently recording
what this field was called and where
the houses Gogor, Dalar, Penrhyn
stood, pursuing echoes that persist
through five hundred years of rival litanies —   610
wild men, pirates, peasant farmers and committees
of academic experts. The field known still
as Bryn Baglau, where the rival bishops
watched Lleuddad thrust their staffs into
dry earth to show how at his word dead wood   615
might cleave together and grow whole
into a great branched tree bursting into leaf,
she found recorded both in Latin and Old Welsh.

Jane's geese, twelve spell-trapped princes,
turn stately silver in procession   620
to standing water where they taste the moon.

Pinched in the jaws of adolescence
a town kid gutting his catch of pollack on the shore
pauses in wonder at the phosphorescence
(sparks of cold fire) flaking from his fingers.
Discarded guts lie shards of pearl.

Athene Noctua hunts in the hayfields.
Her eyes are living stones of yellow light.

So many deaths, too small for us to hear.
The sifted count of one year's remains
below the kestrel roost in the ruined tower
reads like a mediaeval banquet: five dunnock,
fifty-seven wrens, four dozen goldcrest,
a score of robins. And a hundred others.

Then true dark rules, with falling stars
but thresholds are unguarded, left unlocked.

As each beam strokes over them
the blind white shoulders of Lizzie's stone
calm-shrug in answer where they crouch
by the graveyard wall looking back to the lighthouse.

The long waves sing as they run home to find
smooth grey nests they have scooped in the land.

Once, returning from the mainland, beery, late
over a sea slow-flowing as magma
with shadows lying like tar or oil
the sun in its bubble of burning gas
roared too far away for us to hear
and the island, the home we were aiming for
looked a black hole in a world of fire —
an Ithaca of unlost welcomes, our many-sided icon
where time is still unfolding
and where however close we look
the chaos is in harmony.

In a glance at the sky, mind joins the dots:
Orion swings his bright trapeze, Cae'r Gwydion   655
swirls, froth unwinding
on a cosmic tide.

The tiny power of choosing where to be
lends us the dignity of moth or swallow
stream-reading eel, or shearwater   660
learning the whirl of stars
letting them focus its hunger.

In the dark between the flashes
perhaps sometimes we remember
how far, how long light   665
has been travelling to touch us.

Where there is neither
speech nor language, I will make darkness
light before them...

At moonset, as we sleep, the shearwaters   670
waiting off the south-west in their rafts
will surge rowdy and triumphant home
over sea splashed with stars, a glitter of shed scales.

Notes

I hope the work can be read without worrying over who is who, but the details below may clarify or be of interest.

The titles of each section, *Lauds, Prime, Sext, None,* etc., are the "hours" of saying Divine Office and are taken from *The Holy Office.*

l.15 *Benlli:* King of Powys, possibly Irish, who has given his name also to Moel Fenlli in the Clwydian range and Bod Enlli in Anglesey. After an attempt by Garmon to convert him to Christianity (but possibly unrelated to it) he was defeated in an uprising led by Cadell in 474. The island's Welsh name may be connected; the more usual derivation is "island in the current".

l.16 *Garmon:* linked with Pen Llyn (Abersoch church, Llanarmon) but I have invented the story of his coming to the island.

l.42 *Tanwg, Maelrhys, Hywyn, Cadfan:* all "confessors", holy men who are associated with the early church on Bardsey.

l.64 *Kim:* Kim Atkinson, M.A, artist who lives on the island.

l.96 *Lleuddad:* succeeded Cadfan as abbot in the sixth century and is still commemorated in the name of one of the fields near the chapel — Gerddi Lleuddad (Lleuddad's Gardens.)

l.97 *Book of Llandâf:* a 12th century manuscript containing accounts of various saints and a touch of "hype" in its description of Enlli as "the Rome of Britain", twenty thousand saints, etc.

l.129 *Rachel:* sometime Trust gardener who has lived in Nant Barn.

l.134 *Arthur:* with his wife Jane (see l.619) has farmed at Tŷ Pella since 1972.

l.208 *Elgar, Master Caradoc:* This "wise hermit" visited the island about 1105 and recorded the story of Elgar who lived and died alone "unknown to men". See 'Sevens'.

l.229 *Sister:* Helen Mary, S.L.G., who lived a contemplative life on the island from the mid-Seventies until ill-health forced a return to her community in Oxford in 1992.

l.246 *the twins:* Urien and Saiorse, part of the family from the Bird Observatory at Cristin. Meg (l. 372) is their mother.

l.251 *Susan:* Susan Cowdy, President of the Bardsey Island Trust.

l.255 *Lucy:* Lucy Rees, writer. Author of *The Horse's Mind* and a Radio Wales documentary *Tracking Down Wales,* which started on Bardsey.

l.288 *Dyfrig:* 7th century bishop, greatly revered, perhaps the "Confessor Greit" or fervent confessor referred to in the story of Elgar. Exhumed on May 23rd, 1120 and "translated" to the new Llandaf Cathedral.

l.313 *Supply* is the name given for the island boat which sank just off Trwyn Fynwent (Graveyard Point) on November 30th, 1822 with the loss of six lives. The other fourteen people aboard managed to scramble on to the rocks, though they were battered by the swell. The girl mentioned was Sudne Williams, twenty-one year old daughter of the boatman, Thomas Williams of Plas Bach, who was also drowned. Both are buried in Aberdaron.

l.328 German U-boat sunk off Solfach on Christmas Day, 1917.

l.344 *Dic the stonemason*: Richard Williams, Llanfair, who restored much of the walling round the chapel and abbey. Father of Hâf Meredydd, present Trust Secretary.

l.368 the reference is to the rents payable to the Canons of Bardsey from properties in the townships of Issely and Uwchsely (now part of Aberdaron) on the mainland.

l.442 *the dyrnwr*: machine used for chaffing oats, young gorse, etc. as animal feed, driven by a shaft from a horse gin (churning was also done in this way.)

l.453 *Nellie*: Nellie Evans, wife of Wil who farmed on the island 1932-72. Until 1994 she spent each summer in the Old School.

l.490 *Carolyn*: Carolyn Tschering, né Pratt: warden of the Observatory in 1960.

l.515: details from Bardsey Bird and Field Observatory report.

l.517 *Prof*: a not-disrespectful nickname for Dr Dick Loxton.

l.573 *Storws*: the traditional name for the building now more usually called the boathouse. Almost certainly built by Trinity House when they blasted the Cafn entrance as part of the lighthouse development 1816-21.

l.585 *Tŷ Gwydryn*: the House of Glass where Merlin is supposed to have hidden the Thirteen Treasures of Britain. I cannot trace this legend further than Lady Charlotte Guest's 1838 *Mabinogion*.

l.602 *Gwydion*: Gwydion Morley, who has worked for the Bardsey Island Trust as warden since 1988. Also the magician in the Mabinogion story of Blodeuwedd for whom Cae'r Gwydion, the Milky Way, is named. (1.655)

l.604 *Gwen*: Gwen Robson, daughter of Stanley Davies, associated with the island since 1930 when she came as a child to stay with Ifan and Nell Williams at Carreg. For many years she and her husband David were tenants at Plas Bach; each summer they scythed the bracken on the 'Lord's Path' to the top of Mynydd Enlli and collected more of the old island names and stories.

l.606 *Wil*: William Evans, Tŷ Pella. He died in 1979.

l.627 *Athene Noctua*: the Little Owl, very common on Bardsey.

l.638 *Lizzie's stone*: the white gravestone in memory of a lightkeeper's wife.

Acknowledgements

Some of these poems have appeared in the following journals: *Poetry Wales*, *The New Welsh Review*, *Planet*, *The Oxford Magazine* and in publications from The Poetry book Society/Hutchinson, Carcanet and North Western University Press, Illinois.

Acknowledgements are also due to the Welsh Arts Council for assistance in the form of a bursary to get this collection under way.